W9-CPC-934

BEER COCKTAILS

Howard & Ashley Stelzer

*50 superbly crafted
cocktails that liven up your
lagers and ales*

The Harvard Common Press
Boston, Massachusetts

3 4858 00424 4498

WESTERLY PUBLIC LIBRARY
44 Broad St.
Westerly, RI 02891
www.westerlylibrary.org

For Professor Sheehan

The Harvard Common Press
535 Albany Street, Boston, Massachusetts 02118
www.harvardcommonpress.com

Copyright © 2012 by Howard Stelzer and Ashley Stelzer
Photographs © 2012 by Jerry Errico

All rights reserved. No part of this publication may be reproduced or transmitted
in any form or by any means, electronic or mechanical, including photocopying,
recording, or any information storage or retrieval system, without permission in
writing from the publisher.

Printed in China
Printed on acid-free paper

Library of Congress Cataloging-in-Publication Data
Stelzer, Howard.
  Beer Cocktails : 50 superbly crafted cocktails that liven up your lagers and ales /
Howard Stelzer, Ashley Stelzer.
      p. cm. – (50 recipes series)
  Includes index.
  ISBN 978-1-55832-731-3 (hardback)
  1. Cocktails. 2. Beer. I. Stelzer, Ashley. II. Title.
  TX951.S798 2012
  641.2'3--dc23
                                   2011039026

Special bulk-order discounts are available on this and other Harvard Common
Press books. Companies and organizations may purchase books for premiums or
resale, or may arrange a custom edition, by contacting the Marketing Director at
the address above.

Book design by Elizabeth Van Itallie
Photography by Jerry Errico
Drink styling by Chris Lanier

641.23
S

10 9 8 7 6 5 4 3 2 1

CONTENTS

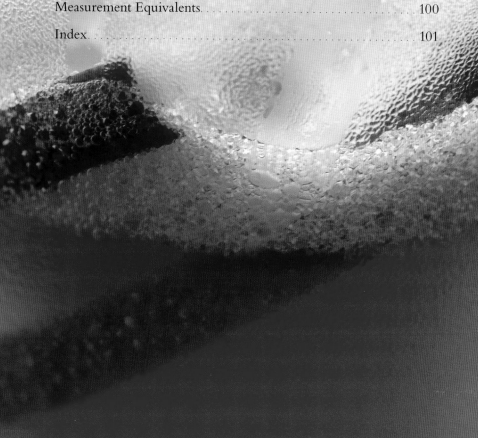

ACKNOWLEDGMENTS

Thank you to all of our friends and family who offered ideas, tasted recipes, and generally encouraged our inappropriate behavior during the writing of this book. Particular thanks to our good pal Jay Sullivan, head brewer at Cambridge Brewing Company, for offering thoughts and expert advice along the way. Thanks also to Jonathan Coleclough and Brian Preston-Campbell for sharing their own beer cocktail exploration notes. Cheers! *Merci* to Eben Freeman, director of bar operations and innovation for AltaMarea Group in New York City, upon whose recipe we based the Bloodied Belgian. *Dank u wel* to Terry Raley at Holland House in Nashville, and to Paul Clarke. We extend expressions of gratitude toward our fellow liquid travelers A.J. Rathbun, Fred Thompson, and Paul Abercrombie for setting a good example. Thanks to Bruce Shaw, head honcho at The Harvard Common Press, for his enthusiastic support and encouragement, and of course to our editor, Valerie Cimino. Further thanks to everyone at HCP for making it all possible. These friends and enablers also deserve a drink or two: Terryl Montgomery (for all the pilsner glasses!), Elizabeth Brash, Teryn Williams, Carrie Holmes Siegel, Christine Merlo, Darren Hutson, Preston Reed, Jerry Spindel, Vicki Milstein, Sandy and LeeAnn Brash, Eagranie Yuh, Peter Perez, Pete Swanson, Benny Nelson, Jason Lescalleet, Vic Rawlings, Elizabeth Witte, Greg Kelley, and Christina Divoll. *L'chaim*, y'all!

INTRODUCTION

It's quite possible that beer is the world's perfect beverage.

In his book *Radical Brewing* (Brewers Publications, 2004), Randy Mosher claims that waiting for grain to ferment is what tempted prehistoric nomads in the Fertile Crescent to settle down in one place. That tale, if you believe it, places beer at the center of the start of modern civilization.

Whatever one's take on Mosher's wistful interpretation of history (we're pretty sure there were some additional factors), it is true that beer has been with us for thousands of years. People enjoyed the product of fermented grain in water before the invention of bread. From Mesopotamia and ancient Egypt (where it was used as medicine), beer spread outward across the world. Brewers could be found in medieval Europe and China; explorers and travelers brought beer across the ocean to the Americas, to Africa, Australia, and New Zealand, and to nearly every country on Earth. Over time, the humble beverage evolved into an astonishing variety of styles shaped by diverse cultures and native ingredients.

Here in America, beer went through major changes in a relatively short amount of time. Most beer before the 1800s was ale, which means that because of the yeast brewers used, it fermented at a warm temperature for just a few weeks. The Industrial Revolution at the end of the nineteenth century brought with it the development of paler malt, pilsner lager, commercial refrigeration, and machines that could perform parts of the brewing process automatically on a large scale. With those advancements came beers that could stay fresh for longer and ship far away with less risk of spoiling. Technology effectively created competition for small local brewers.

In the early twentieth century, the Eighteenth Amendment temporarily halted large-scale beer production, but it also made home brewing illegal. When it was repealed in 1933, industrial brewing returned to the United States, but brewing beer at home remained a crime. That didn't change until 1978. In the intervening years, Americans' access to beer was quite limited. National brands such as Anheuser-Busch grew during that time, marketing and selling homogeneous products designed to appeal to the most people possible across the widest expanse of demographics and geography. These very pale beers, watered down further with adjuncts (additions) like rice, effectively replaced America's regional and local styles as the popular favorites. For most American beer drinkers during that time, anything other than these lagers was suspiciously unfamiliar.

Thankfully, the legalization of home brewing also sparked a wave of independent brewpubs and microbrewers. The steadily growing availability of different kinds of beer increased the demand for imports as Americans rediscovered beer. Home brewers began to experiment freely with the new diversity of styles now accessible to them. Interest in noncorporate beer began to surge. The Anchor Steam Brewing Company made a big, early impact by reviving steam beer, a uniquely American style once popular in San Francisco, inspiring other home brewers to go pro as well.

We now live in an age in which curious thrill-seeking drinkers can seek out and sample beer from just about anywhere in the world. One used to have to travel to the pubs in England to sample the local brew or visit a Belgian abbey to try the legendary beer made by Trappist monks. Today, geography is not an obstacle. Creative brewers in Tokyo are making American-style India pale ales; a Colorado brewery specializes in Belgian styles; Russian brewers are making German-style *maibock*; brewers in Seattle are tweaking English styles using hops from the Pacific Northwest; and the list goes on. It isn't uncommon to find at least a small sampling of beers from Germany, the UK, Canada, and a few American regions in your average corner store or supermarket. The changes are coming with remarkable speed. As recently as ten years ago, the taps of most bars, even in a beer-conscious city like Boston (where we live), offered only the big national brands. Nowadays, you'd be hard pressed to find a bar that *doesn't* offer at least a couple of local brewers' products. Beer pairing is becoming as common as wine pairing at dinner. This all points in one direction: More and more people are demanding better beer.

Which brings us to . . . beer cocktails.

BEER BASICS

So, now that we've established that beer is a delicious, historically and culturally significant beverage, why would you want to add anything to it? Don't we owe those hard-working brewers the respect of enjoying their creations in as pure a form as possible? To that rhetorical question, well-intentioned and naively sentimental though it may be, we say: nonsense. Beer is deserving of respect and appreciation, but no liquid is sacred in the world of cocktails. Cocktails are as creative a culinary expression as any other, and the best drinks demand excellent ingredients. In fact, anyone who mixes a drink is

already drawing upon high-quality creations to build something new. Just as you might mix a fine bourbon into a Manhattan or a small-batch gin into an Aviation, so can and should you mix quality beers into great cocktails. With all the combinations of flavors and textures in the world, there is no reason to limit our libations and not play with beer as an ingredient. Camper English, writing about beer cocktails at Epicurious.com, put it quite well: "Many beer enthusiasts, like oenophiles and Scotch lovers, believe in the purity of their drink and don't welcome dilutions. Let them live in their gated communities."

Ah, but we can still hear the skeptics and purists grumbling about beer being somehow off limits to creative cocktailery. If our plea for open-mindedness behind the bar has not yet convinced you, let us try another tack: History is not on your side. Beer cocktails predate the craft beer movement and even the modern cocktail. They're already here, folks! Back in colonial Massachusetts, bartenders were making warm ale flips to bring cheer to otherwise bleak New England winters (see page 94 for an authentic recipe). What we know today as a Radler originated in the Bavarian mountains more than a century ago (skip ahead to page 35 for recipes and variations). Mexico's *cerveza preparada* is of uncertain origin, but food writer Colman Andrews researched its most famous iteration, the Michelada, for *Gourmet* magazine and concluded that the drink probably dates back to the 1940s.

Still wary of seemingly unbeerlike ingredients mingling with your precious brew? Consider this: That flavor you most associate with beer was, for centuries, not nearly as ubiquitous as it is today. Hops, the pungent flower clusters that give modern beer its familiar bitterness and aroma, didn't really catch on until the late 1600s. Before then, beer was flavored with dandelion, burdock root, mint, hay, crab claws, and oyster shells, as well as all manner of herbs, roots, fruits, and spices. Hops are a significant part of beer history because of their preservative qualities, but they're far from the only flavor used for beer. Modern craft brewers like Dogfish Head and Samuel Smith have dipped into history for inspiration; so too can we look to beer's history of creative flavor combinations to create new cocktails.

The unavoidable fact is that as more drinkers are seeking beer, more bartenders are exploring beer as an ingredient in their cocktails. From the trendy, cutting-edge cocktail bars of New York City to the beer mecca of Portland, Oregon (where the Hop and Vine bar hosts Brewing Up Cocktails, an annual beer cocktail event, as part of July's Oregon Craft Beer Month), the country's top drink slingers are using beer as a key component in creating new libations. Beer provides effervescence to a cocktail, much like sparkling wine or club soda, but with an entirely different flavor profile. The bitterness of hops can be balanced with sweet or spicy. The herbs, fruits, and spices in many craft beers and traditional seasonal styles lend themselves to all kinds of flavor possibilities.

If you *still* need convincing, just ask yourself this question: Am I the sort of person who enjoys things that taste good? If you're not sure, please take a long, hard look in the mirror and try to remember why you bothered to wake up this morning. Everyone else, come along with us!

THINGS YOU NEED TO KNOW BEFORE YOU BEGIN

Before you mix your first beer cocktail, let's talk about what goes into beer in the first place.

How Beer Is Made

Beer is made from grain, yeast, water, and some flavoring agent, which is usually hops. The grain is allowed to sprout just a bit, then it's kiln dried, roasted, or stewed wet, depending on what kind of malt the brewer wants. The degree to which the grain is roasted will determine the color and some of the flavor of the beer. As with coffee, a darker roast yields a darker product. Next, the malted grain is mixed with water to create a *mash*, which breaks down the starch in the grain into sugars. The resulting sugar water is then strained off the grain in a process called *lautering*. At this stage, what you have is not yet beer; it's a clear malty liquid called *wort*.

Once the wort is extracted from the mash, it's brought to a boil. A brewer will then add hops (or some other flavoring agent) to the boiling wort, imparting bitterness and aroma to the brew. There are many different varieties of hops and as many strategies for combining them at different times during the boil as there are beers. Finally, the wort is taken off the heat and stored where the temperature is stable, and then yeast is added.

It is during this stage in the brewing process when fermentation happens. The yeast eats the sugars in the wort, producing our friend alcohol as a byproduct. Like hops, yeast comes in many varieties, each with its own character. There are even brewers, notably those in Belgium, who invite wild yeast strains to come join the process by exposing their wort to the open air, allowing local strains to drift in. Once fermentation has run its course, the beer is strained off the yeast, bottled or kegged, and then consumed.

Types of Beer

Beer can be divided into two main families: ales and lagers. The difference depends on the type of yeast that's used.

The yeast used for ales needs relatively warm temperatures (typically between 60° and 75°F) in order to turn the sugars from the wort into alcohol. They do their work fairly quickly. From the time yeast is added and fermentation begins, ales can be consumed in as little as three or four weeks.

Yeast used for lager, on the other hand, needs more time to ferment at colder temperatures (typically between 46° and 55°F). Lager yeast eats its sugars at the bottom of the fermenter, which is why you'll sometimes hear lagers referred to as *bottom-fermented beer*. Ales could be called *top-fermented beer*, by the same logic. The amount of time that lagers need in order to turn sugar into alcohol is actually how this type of beer got its name. The term *lager* comes from the German word for "storage," so named because thirteenth-century German brewers stored their bottom-fermented beer in caves in the Alps.

It is debatable whether someone can tell a lager from an ale merely by looking at it or tasting it. Some styles of lagers are indeed quite light, like pilsners. But some ales are light, too, such as *kölsch* (which is almost clear) and *hefeweizen*. *Schwarzbier* (literally "black beer") is a dark lager. American reds and doppelbocks are heavy lagers as well. It really comes down to how the beer was made. Beyond that, brewers are immensely creative and have developed styles of both ale and lager that run a wide range of attributes.

BEER STYLES

There are many different styles of both ales and lagers. Some have become classics and are deeply embedded in the culture of the countries where they were first developed. Others have changed over time or have adapted to new brewing technology. Still other styles come about when creative brewers play freely with whatever inspires them. Here's a look at the most commonly known styles of beer.

Pale ale is a broad category of beers, united in their relatively high proportion of pale malts in the brewing process. The color of the malt used will affect the color of the finished beer, so pale malts tend to yield paler ales. One of the most popular kinds of pale ale is the IPA, or India pale ale. English IPAs were created in the eighteenth century for export to British soldiers in India, hence the name. Because of hops' preservative quality, these beers were hoppier than their domestic cousins. A good IPA is pleasantly bitter, crisp, and refreshing. American breweries have taken up the style, adding even more hops to exploit the flavors of domestic varieties. A particularly strong style is called an imperial IPA or double IPA.

Another pale ale that originated in the UK is the extra special bitter, or ESB. This copper-colored ale is less carbonated, with a more pronounced malt flavor.

Belgium has given the world many unique styles of beer, including lambic, *geuze*, and Flemish sour. Lambic and *geuze* are light-bodied styles of ale that acquire their distinctly tart flavors by exposure to wild yeast. They can be flavored with cherries, raspberries, peaches, or cassis, though other fruit can be used as well. Flemish sour ales, also called Flemish reds, are blends made from aged and fresh beers, producing a refreshingly sour, somewhat astringent flavor. An acquired taste, perhaps, but we recommend acquiring it. Belgium also has its own version of an IPA, with high alcohol content and bottle conditioning with Belgian yeast.

Stouts and porters are the darkest ales, but not all of them are heavy or even particularly strong. The most popular stout in the world, Guinness, is dry, with a relatively light body and low alcohol level. Brewers in the UK and the United States, notably Samuel Smith and Founders, have come up with exemplary full-bodied stouts brewed with oatmeal and espresso. Creative brewers have upped the alcohol with imperial stouts, sweetened them with chocolate, and have even used oysters as a flavoring.

There is much debate within the beer world over what the difference is between stout and porter. The short answer is: There really isn't one. At the turn of the nineteenth century, stout was simply the term used to describe the strongest porters. But even that hasn't always been the case, as some stouts were made with pale malt, resulting in a pale stout. Today, whichever term is used seems to depend on the brewer's preference. As long as our glass is full, we don't think it matters much.

Barleywine, an English style of ale that has become more popular in America recently, is quite strong and intensely hoppy, with lively citrus notes. Barleywine can range in color from deep amber to mahogany and is typically served in smaller portions due to its high alcohol content and complex flavor. We especially like The Wizard from Short's Brewing Company of Bellaire, Michigan, and Fred from the inimitable Hair of the Dog Brewing Company in Portland, Oregon, but we will happily accept any barleywine you hand to us.

Brown ales originated in England and are generally characterized by lower alcohol content, malty aroma, and medium body. In the United States, the British classic Newcastle Brown Ale is available nationwide, though many regional breweries produce their own version of the style. In New York, Sixpoint Craft Ales' Brownstone is hard to beat. Our local favorite, Saint Botolph's Town by Boston's own Pretty Things Beer & Ale Project, is also wonderful.

The lightest of the lagers are obviously the adjunct-heavy American lagers, which have hardly any hop flavor at all, but there are many other American lagers with fuller flavor, including those by Samuel Adams, Brooklyn, Yuengling, and many others. Germany takes its brewing traditions very seriously, and we're lucky to be able to find several German lagers here in the United States. The most prevalent examples are the *dunkel* (meaning dark) and strong bock styles, both quite popular in the autumn when most right-thinking people head toward the nearest Oktoberfest celebration. We also have access to plenty of good domestic and imported pilsners, including the classic Pilsner Urquell from the Czech Republic.

GLASSWARE

Before you enjoy your cocktail, you will of course need to put your drink into a glass, to avoid a big mess. The most common beer-friendly glasses are the mug, the pint glass, the pilsner glass, the flute, and the goblet. Common cocktail glasses that we'll also use include the Collins glass, the cocktail (or martini) glass, the highball, and the old-fashioned.

Mugs usually hold 16 ounces and feature a wide mouth and a handle. Some folks like to store their beer mugs in the freezer, so that drinks poured into them are instantly frosty.

A pint glass also holds 16 ounces, though imperial pint glasses are slightly larger and hold 20 ounces. An imperial pint is also called a British pint. Either one is somewhat conical, flaring out toward the top. You may find a pint glass with a top section that is straighter. These are called "nonic" pint glasses. A pint glass is shaped the way it is so that a frothy head forms at the top when a beer is poured into it. Some beers, especially those from Belgium, form lovely lace patterns of foam on the sides of the glass. Others, like a Guinness stout, have a wonderful layered appearance with dark ale below and white head at the top if the beer is poured correctly.

Pilsner, the deservingly popular lager that originated in the Czech city of Pilsen, has its own glass. A tall V-shape directs the aroma upward toward the drinker, so that the full hop bouquet can be savored with each sip. For the original beer in this style, try Pilsner Urquell, which has been brewed continuously since 1842.

A flute glass (also called a champagne glass) is typically narrow and tall, with a cylindrical container on top of a short stem. Another type of champagne glass, with a saucer-like bowl, is called a coupe glass.

Goblets are larger bowls on shorter stems. They are used primarily to serve Belgian beers. Sometimes tulip glasses, with their bulbous bodies and flared tops, are used to serve Belgian or Scottish ales.

A Collins glass holds 10 to 14 ounces and has straight sides.

Cocktail (martini) glasses are those iconic 4- to 6-ounce or larger flared cups atop long stems. The bowl has straight sides, in a wide V shape.

The highball is a tall glass with straight sides that typically holds between 8 and 14 ounces.

Old-fashioned glasses are for smaller drinks, generally 4 to 6 ounces. They are stocky, with straight sides and a heavy bottom. There are also double old-fashioned glasses.

TOOLS

Any good home bar should be stocked with more than just glassware and beer. It should also have the right tools. Here are the ones you'll need for most of the drinks in this book:

Bottle opener: Do we really need to explain this one? Beer tends to come in bottles, though cans of quality brew (from brewers like Oskar Blues in Colorado and 21st Amendment in San Francisco) are making inroads. Bottles can have standard bottle caps, though some have corks that require the same sort of corkscrew you'd use to open a bottle of wine. Do not attempt to open anything with your teeth.

Bar spoon: This is a long, skinny spoon with a small bowl for stirring tall drinks that aren't shaken over ice.

Boston shaker: One of the two main varieties of cocktail shakers, this is the type you usually see in bars. It's made up of a steel cone with a mixing glass that fits snugly over it. You must fit them firmly together to make a seal or else you will end up with a mess.

Standard shaker: Unlike the Boston shaker, this version (also called the cobbler shaker) is entirely steel and has a built-in strainer and a little cup on top that can also be used for measuring. This variety is generally easier to use than the Boston shaker.

Hawthorne strainer: If you have a Boston shaker, you will also need one of these little wire-rimmed strainers in order to strain out the contents.

Citrus stripper/zester: Use this little tool for stripping peel from fresh citrus to use as garnish.

Muddler: This is a wooden or metal pestle-like tool that you will use to muddle, or crush, fruits and herbs before adding the liquids.

SIMPLE SYRUP

Several of the drinks in this book call for simple syrup. We suggest making a batch of this and keeping it in your fridge. It won't go bad, and having it on hand is much more convenient than making new syrup every time you need some. The recipe couldn't be easier: Bring 1 part sugar and 1 part water (whatever quantities you think you will go through in a reasonable amount of time) to a boil in a saucepan. Stir often, until all the sugar is dissolved. Remove from the heat and allow the syrup to cool. Put it in an airtight container and store it in the refrigerator.

Some of our recipes call for simple syrup that's been infused with additional flavoring. We use vanilla bean seeds, star anise pods, and peeled fresh ginger, all of which should be added to the syrup just after it comes off the heat. Refrigerate the syrup overnight, then strain out the spices and refrigerate in an airtight container.

2

LAGER
Than Life
(OR, A WHITER SHADE OF PALE)

The Frank Booth • Sloe Work Day • Root Beer • Cheveux de Conan • Lager Grog • KnickerTwister • Boilermaker • Maru • Skippy • Radler • Snakebite • Michelada • Ale Punch • Waldmeister

This chapter features cocktails made with relatively light-bodied beers. Some of these drinks are based on the most popular beers in America, the light, adjunct-heavy lagers made by mega-corporations (Budweiser, Coors, Pabst, and so forth). These provide excellent carbonation when mixed with other ingredients and are light enough not to overwhelm the flavors of fruit and spirits.

We also include here drinks made using medium-bodied pale ales and wheat beers. Pale ales tend to be bitter and strongly hoppy, which means you have to be careful when mixing them into cocktails. They need something herbal to blend with them, or else the hop flavor can take over. Wheat beers are light and fruity and perfect for summertime coolers. They have a natural affinity for citrus, and when served on their own are typically accompanied by a squeeze of lemon or orange.

THE **FRANK** BOOTH

Serves 2

The Frank Booth, a sort-of classic from the seedy under-belly of the Pacific Northwest, emphatically demands Pabst Blue Ribbon. If you can't get PBR for some reason, any light American lager will work. Just remember: Whatever you do, don't ever make this drink with Heineken. Trust us.

Ice cubes
2 ounces whiskey
1 ounce freshly squeezed lime juice
10 ounces Pabst Blue Ribbon or similar light American lager
Lime wedges, for garnish

1. Fill a cocktail shaker halfway full with ice cubes. Add the whiskey and lime juice and shake well.

2. Strain into two old-fashioned glasses. Top each with half of the PBR. Garnish each with a lime wedge, and serve.

" Beer should be enjoyed with the right mixture of abandon and restraint."
—M.F.K. FISHER

SLOE WORK DAY

Serves 1

Y'know, our day jobs are pretty intense. We don't ever have days when we're not extremely, nonstop busy. We like it that way. But we remember when we had regular desk jobs, and sometimes . . . well, sometimes it was just a slow day. Those days were kinda nice. We could breathe, clean our cubicle, and finally get to those tasks we put off because we were just too darn busy. Since we don't have days like that anymore, we invented a slow work day of our own. This drink has a gorgeous deep purple color and a pleasing dryness that respects the flavors of the IPA. We think it's delicious, and now it's official: Sloe Work Day was declared the winner of the Summer 2011 "Brew Something New" Craft Beer Cocktail Contest, held at Scholars American Bistro and Cocktail Lounge in Boston!

Ice cubes
2 ounces blackberry puree (see Note)
1½ ounces sloe gin
¾ ounce St-Germain elderflower liqueur
½ ounce freshly squeezed lemon juice
4 ounces India pale ale
1 mint sprig, for garnish

1. Fill a cocktail shaker halfway full with ice cubes. Add the blackberry puree, sloe gin, St-Germain, and lemon juice. Shake well.

2. Strain into a Collins glass. Top with the IPA, garnish with the mint sprig, and serve.

NOTE • Whir 1 cup fresh blackberries in your blender to yield 2 ounces puree. If fresh blackberries aren't in season, either frozen berries or frozen puree will work nicely here.

ROOT BEER

Serves 1

Root liqueur plus beer equals Root Beer. The amaretto gives this drink nuttiness and extra kick. We love Root, a strongly herbal liqueur, but substitute root beer schnapps if you can't find Root in your area. You'll want to use a light American lager for this drink, such as Miller Genuine Draft or Pabst Blue Ribbon. If you desire a stronger flavor, try it with Pilsner Urquell.

⅓ ounce amaretto
⅔ ounce Root liqueur
11 ounces lager

Add the amaretto and Root to a chilled 12-ounce pilsner glass. Top with lager to fill the glass. Stir gently, and serve.

❝ The government will fail that raises the price of beer." —Czech proverb

CHEVEUX DE **CONAN**

Serves 1

This one is named for our favorite ginger, Mr. Conan O'Brien. We like this with Rogue Irish Lager or Harp, or something else relatively light.

Ice cubes
1 ounce bourbon
Juice of 1 lemon
1½ ounces honey
½ ounce Domaine de Canton ginger liqueur
6 ounces lager
2 or 3 thin slices fresh ginger, for garnish

1. Fill a cocktail shaker halfway full with ice cubes. Add the bourbon, lemon juice, honey, and ginger liqueur to the shaker and shake to blend.

2. Put two large ice cubes into a double old-fashioned glass, and strain the drink into the glass. Top with the lager, garnish with the ginger, and serve.

LAGER GROG

Serves 4

In honor of our beloved hometown, this warm cocktail uses Samuel Adams's flagship Boston Lager for a malty, somewhat sweet drink that will thaw the bones of anyone trying to make it through a brutal New England winter.

12 ounces Samuel Adams Boston Lager
4 ounces apple cider
3 ounces freshly squeezed orange juice
2 ounces cream sherry
2 ounces orange liqueur, such as Grand Marnier
1 ounce amaretto
1 orange, sliced
4 whole cloves
2 star anise pods

1. Add all of the ingredients to a medium saucepan and heat over low heat until warm.

2. Remove and reserve the orange slices for garnish. Strain the mixture into four Irish coffee mugs, straining out the star anise and cloves. Add the orange slices and serve warm.

KNICKERTWISTER

Serves 1

The hop flavor of the IPA blends remarkably with the allspice dram in this variation on the classic Knickerbocker. We like it with Victory HopDevil, but Harpoon IPA or Lagunitas IPA would be equally delicious.

Ice cubes
1 ounce dry vermouth
1 ounce sweet vermouth
½ ounce St. Elizabeth Allspice Dram
Dash of orange bitters
2 ounces India pale ale
1 lemon twist, for garnish

1. Fill a mixing glass halfway full with ice cubes. Add the vermouths, allspice dram, and orange bitters, and stir.

2. Strain into a chilled cocktail glass. Top with the IPA. Run the lemon twist around the rim, twist it into the drink, and drop it in. Serve immediately.

" Beer does not make itself properly by itself. It takes an element of mystery and of things that no one can understand."
—FRITZ MAYTAG, BREWER

BOILERMAKER

Serves 1

The boilermaker is a real macho drink, made using just two ingredients: a beer and a spirit. The fun is all in the presentation, as well as in the ritual of consuming it. A boilermaker should be swallowed in one big thirsty gulp. It's been the star of many a wild party, and probably the end of even more. The recipe, such as it is, is so simple that it hardly merits writing out in standard recipe form, but we'll do that just as a formality and for consistency's sake.

16 ounces American light lager, such as Bud, Pabst, or Yuengling
1 shot glass full of whiskey

Pour the very cold beer into a frosty pint glass or beer mug. Drop the shot of whiskey—including the glass!—into the beer, and then quickly chug the entire thing. When we say quickly, we mean it . . . drink this slowly and you've both missed the point of a Boilermaker and opened yourself up to the ridicule of all those so-called friends who peer-pressured you into this foolishness in the first place. Just be careful about the shot glass hitting your teeth.

VARIATION • *The Boilermaker* is named for the tough men and women who work with heavy machinery and could no doubt make it look easy to down one of these. One variation calls for serving the whiskey on the side and drinking each element separately, or for chasing a shot of whiskey with the beer in a separate glass. But that defeats the showy point of the entire enterprise. Other versions call for dropping rum, vodka, or even tequila into your beer. We prefer a shot of bourbon (one of the big guys, like Jim Beam or Jack Daniel's) dropped into a crisp, light American beer such as Pabst Blue Ribbon or Yuengling. In Korea, the popular variation among the after-work crowd is the Poktanju, which calls for dropping a shot of soju (a sweet, vodka-like spirit) into a glass of lager.

MARU

Serves 4

Maru is the name of the adorable Japanese cat whose love of jumping into and out of boxes has inspired us to waste many happy hours drinking beer in front of our computer when we should have been working instead. This cocktail has the popular Japanese lager Sapporo as its base, a crisp and well-carbonated brew that is typically paired with sushi. Here, the slight bitterness of the beer is tempered by tart berries and mandarin oranges.

12 fresh blackberries
Ice cubes
4 ounces freshly squeezed mandarin orange juice
3 ounces St-Germain elderflower liqueur
2 ounces Chambord
12 ounces Sapporo

1. Muddle the blackberries in the bottom of a cocktail shaker. Fill the shaker halfway full with ice cubes, add the mandarin orange juice, Chambord, and St-Germain, and shake vigorously.

2. Strain into four goblets or wine glasses, top with the Sapporo, and serve.

SKIPPY

Serves 10

A college party drink, this is typically prepared by emptying an awfully large quantity of each ingredient into a plastic-lined trash can. Guests help themselves by dunking a plastic cup into the can and . . . well, you'd be more apt to try this if I told you what they call it in France: a *Panaché! Très* classy, *non?* The Skippy is similar to a Radler (page 35), but with vodka added to get you addled. Serve it in a large bowl at a party (*please* not a trash can, even if it's clean). Thanks to our pal Muñoz for extensive research and testing of this one.

8 ounces vodka
16 ounces chilled American light lager, such as Miller Genuine Draft
   or Budweiser
16 ounces chilled sparkling lemonade
Lemon slices, for garnish

Add the vodka, lager, and lemonade to a large chilled punch bowl and stir. Garnish with lemon slices. To serve, ladle into chilled punch glasses.

   " Sam: What would you like, Normie?
Norm: A reason to live. Give me another beer." —TED DANSON AND GEORGE WENDT, FROM *CHEERS*

RADLER

Serves 1

This drink is immensely popular in the mountains of Germany and Austria, but let's try to make it go international. The bicyclists (*die radler*, natch) of Bavaria rely on their mix of *weissbier* and lemon-lime soda for a refreshing pause in their two-wheeled treks across steep terrain. It has just enough alcohol to cheer the soul, but not so much as to lead one radlering off a cliff into the canyons below. *Ach, mein gott!*

Lemon-lime soda? Really? *Zitronenlimonade*, a fizzy soft drink, is what was used by Franz Xaver Kugler when he first invented it in 1922 as a way to stretch his limited beer supply to serve a large number of bicyclists stopping by his saloon. While there have been countless iterations and reinventions of the Radler since then, lemon-lime soda is the classic. You want a bit of extra carbonation to keep your Radler light enough for a midday tipple. This isn't the drink you pound back with pals until the pubs close. It's really intended to cool you down and leave you in good enough shape to carry on with your radling.

8 ounces *weissbier*, such as Weihenstephaner, Hacker-Pschorr,
    or Julius Echter
8 ounces lemon-lime soda
Lemon wedge
Lime wedge

Combine both liquids in a pilsner glass and serve. Squeeze the lemon and lime wedges into the glass, to taste. Drink, smile, repeat.

VARIATIONS • *Kante Ente:* This is from Thuringia, in central Germany. Fill a pilsner glass two-thirds full of pilsner. Top it off with lemon-lime soda and a shot of cherry Heering. Exact measurements aren't important here, so experiment and make it to your taste.
• *Broadway:* Another drink in the Shandy family, this one is made with equal parts lager and cola. It's popular in Japan.

SNAKEBITE

Serves 1

Use Magners or Strongbow cider if you want to be traditional for this classic English beer cocktail, but there are many fine dry American ciders as well. For the beer, try Harp, Stella Artois, or anything with a flavor that won't overwhelm the apple. The Snakebite is part of the Shandy (or Shandygaff) family of drinks, made by combining one part beer with one part other beverage, typically something carbonated.

Former President Bill Clinton was famously refused a Snakebite when he ordered one at the Old Bell Tavern in Harrogate, North Yorkshire, in 2001. The bartender claimed that it was illegal to serve and that he might lose his license if he poured one for the ex-president. Clinton reportedly replied, "That's a shame. It would have brought out my true personality."

In reality, Snakebites are not illegal, but bartenders of a more cautious nature have been known to avoid the inevitable trouble caused by enthusiastic overconsumption by simply inventing a prohibition by which they insist they must abide. Luckily, a Snakebite is very easy to make at home.

8 ounces hard cider
8 ounces lager

Fill a pint glass halfway with the cider, then top with the lager. Tilt back, then repeat until you are unable to continue doing so.

VARIATION • *Bee Sting:* Sub in orange juice for the cider, then top with an equal quantity of porter.

MICHELADA

Serves 1

We suggest making this classic Mexican beer cocktail with Mexican lager for the sake of authenticity. Look for the chile-lime seasoning combo at Latin markets or in the Latin foods aisle of your local supermarket.

Generous pinch of coarse salt
Generous pinch of chile-lime seasoning
1 lime wedge
Ice cubes
2 tablespoons freshly squeezed lime juice
Tabasco sauce, to taste
Dash of Worcestershire sauce
12 ounces Dos Equis or Corona

1. Combine the salt and chile-lime seasoning on a small plate. Moisten the rim of a pint glass with the lime wedge, then dip the rim to coat it with the salt and seasoning.

2. Fill the glass with ice cubes, then add the lime juice, Tabasco, and Worcestershire sauce. Top with the beer, and sprinkle a small amount of the salt and seasoning on top. Serve.

VARIATIONS • #1: For additional authenticity, use Maggi Seasoning instead of Worcestershire sauce.

•#2: If the Tabasco is too vinegary for you, try experimenting with other spicy sauces, but take care not to overpower with brutal fire. The heat should be an accent to a Michelada, not the dominant flavor.

•#3: The *Chelada* is a variation on the Michelada, but there's some controversy about the actual difference between the two drinks. To us, a Chelada is a Michelada with the addition of either tomato juice or Clamato (a tomato-clam juice blend available in many supermarkets). Garnish with celery sticks. A Chelada is considered the Mexican version of the Bloody Mary. So what's the controversy? Well, some say that a Michelada is the drink that always contains tomato juice and that the Chelada *never* does. Others say the exact opposite. We're not going to settle the argument, but we'll mull it over while we drink a couple of each.

ALE **PUNCH**

Serves 12

Having a dozen of your closest pals over on a crisp autumn evening? This slightly herbal, not too sweet punch will please even the most finicky of party guests. Sierra Nevada works nicely.

32 ounces chilled pale ale
4 ounces brandy
4 ounces dry or sweet sherry
4 ounces St. Elizabeth Allspice Dram
4 ounces simple syrup (page 19)
2 ounces freshly squeezed lemon juice

Combine all the ingredients in a large chilled punch bowl. To serve, ladle into chilled punch glasses.

> Give beer to those who are perishing, wine to those who are in anguish. Let them drink and forget their poverty and remember their misery no more." —PROVERBS 31:6

WALD**MEISTER**

Serves 1

A classic old German beer cocktail, the Waldmeister (also known as *Berliner Weisse mit Waldmeister*) is named for its main flavoring, a forest-growing herb that's called woodruff in English. The drink is a relative of the Radler, though it has its roots in *gruitbier,* or "fruit beer," which predates the use of hops as a flavoring agent. When you fix Waldmeisters for your pals on a balmy summer day, you'll experience what it was like to cool off with a cold brew in medieval Europe. You can purchase woodruff syrup from www.germandeli.com.

16 ounces Berliner *Weissbier*, or any German or German-style *weisse*
1½ ounces woodruff syrup

Pour the cold beer into a wide, stemmed glass, such as a red wine goblet, then quickly stir in the syrup. As a variation, you can serve this unstirred, with a long spoon provided so that the recipient can stir the drink him- or herself.

VARIATIONS • *Berliner Weisse Spezial:* Follow the directions above, adding a shot of crème de cassis.
• *Frühstück Weisse ("Breakfast Beer"):* Use 8 ounces *Weissbier* and ³/₄ ounce woodruff syrup, and top it off with freshly squeezed orange juice.
• *Himbeere (Raspberry):* Use raspberry syrup (also available from www. germandeli.com, though any raspberry syrup will do in a pinch) instead of the woodruff. Garnish with a couple of fresh raspberries.

3

ABBEY ROAD

(OR, TRAPPIST IN THE CLOSET)

Belgian 75 • Bloodied Belgian • Belgian 125 • Sympathy for the Devil • De Pêche à la Mode • Witte • Root Beer Float • The Retiree • Appaloosa • Sing Sing Sling • Joe Pêche • Myrna Loy

Ask any serious beer geek where the greatest beers in the world come from, and the most likely answer is Belgium. In contrast to its neighbor Germany, where strict *Reinheitsgebot* "purity" laws govern precisely which ingredients Deutsche *brauereien* are allowed to use, the Belgians are known for taking exciting risks with fruit additives, wild yeast, sour and tart flavors, and more. Belgian Trappist monks in particular have a tradition of brewing stellar beers for their communities and to fund their monasteries. Beers made outside of monasteries but in the Trappist style are called abbey beers. When we traveled through Belgium on our honeymoon, we tried as many beers as we could but were only able to scratch the surface. We'll return someday to continue exploring.

For this chapter, we were inspired to create drinks that honor the unique flavors of Belgian beer. If you cannot find Belgian beer where you live, you may see American beers made in Belgian styles, which are becoming increasingly common. New Belgium (in Colorado), Ommegang (in upstate New York), and Russian River (in Northern California) are particularly successful at making top-quality American interpretations, though there are many other breweries worth investigating. Follow your own tastes and experiment with what is available. Or just hop on a flight to Bruges! If you do that, please contact us first so that we can give you a list of beers we'd like you to bring back for us. Thanks in advance.

BELGIAN **75**

Serves 1

Here's our version of the classic gin cocktail the French 75, made using (you guessed it) Belgian beer, in this case a high-alcohol golden ale.

Ice cubes
1 ounce gin
½ ounce freshly squeezed lemon juice
1 teaspoon sugar
5 ounces Duvel, Kwak, Delirium Tremens, or a similar Belgian pale ale
1 orange twist, for garnish

1. Fill a cocktail shaker halfway full with ice cubes. Add the gin, lemon juice, and sugar, and shake.

2. Fill a Collins glass halfway full with ice cubes. Strain the mixture into the glass. Slowly top with the ale. Garnish with the orange twist and serve.

> But if at church they would give some ale, and a pleasant fire our souls to regale. We'd sing and we'd pray all the live long day, nor ever once from the church to stray."
> —WILLIAM BLAKE

BLOODIED BELGIAN

Serves 1

Here's a take on the classic Blood and Sand cocktail, using Flemish-style sour ale or *kriek* (which means "cherry") lambic instead of cherry liqueur. Lambic is a distinctively Belgian style of beer, made with wild yeast as opposed to the carefully controlled fermentation of conventional ales. It is often flavored with fruit, such as cherries or raspberries. Thanks to Eben Freeman, who serves a version of this drink at Ai Fiori in New York City.

Ice cubes
¾ ounce Scotch whisky
¾ ounce sweet vermouth
2 ounces freshly squeezed blood orange juice
4 ounces Flemish sour ale or *kriek* lambic
2 fresh cherries, for garnish

1. Fill a cocktail shaker halfway full with ice cubes. Add the Scotch, vermouth, and blood orange juice and shake until blended.
2. Strain into a cocktail glass. Top with the ale, drop in the cherries for garnish, and serve.

BELGIAN 125

Serves 1

Having to choose a favorite kind of beer doesn't seem fair. It's like having to choose a favorite . . . um, what else could be as important as beer? We can't think of anything right now, but you know what we mean. Anyway, if we *had* to choose a favorite, it would be the Flemish style of sour ale made by brewers like Duchesse de Bourgogne and Rodenbach. While a traditional French 125 is made with Cognac and Champagne, we prefer to celebrate happy occasions with a Belgian-inspired twist on the classic.

1 orange
¾ ounce Cognac
5 ounces Flemish sour ale

1. Slice a wheel from the middle of the orange, then juice the remaining halves. Set the wheel aside.

2. Fill a cocktail shaker halfway full with ice cubes. Add the Cognac and orange juice and shake well.

3. Fill a Collins glass halfway full with ice cubes and strain the mixture into the glass. Top with the sour ale, garnish with the reserved orange wheel, and serve.

“ It is a fair wind that blew men to the ale.”
—WASHINGTON IRVING

SYMPATHY **FOR THE DEVIL**

Serves 1

Many have been tempted to make a deal with the devil. Robert Johnson perfected the blues thanks to the dark blessings of the Horned One. And Dr. Faustus did fairly well, for a while. Duvel, a beer named after you-know-who, is a refreshing Belgian ale that packs more of a wallop than one might think at first sip. This recipe heightens the golden strong ale's pleasant bitterness and aromatic spice. It's a lovely and refreshing drink for a warm summer afternoon, especially if you don't have anything important to do that evening.

Absinthe or Pernod
1½ ounces Hendrick's gin
6 ounces Duvel

1. Add a bit of absinthe to an 8-ounce flute glass, swish it around to coat the inside, and pour it out.

2. Add the gin, then fill the rest of the glass with Duvel. Serve immediately.

DE PÊCHE À LA MODE

Serves 2

Our take on the Bellini is much cooler than the original. In fact (wait for it), we *just can't get enough!* Ouch. This is a sweet cooler to help you beat the summer heat. We like using lambic for cocktails because of the ease with which its light, faintly tart flavors blend with spirits and fruity ingredients.

4 scoops vanilla or peach ice cream
4 ounces peach preserves
2 ounces brandy
12 ounces peach lambic, such as Lindemans Pêche

1. Add two scoops of ice cream to each of two chilled mugs. Combine the peach preserves and brandy in a cup, then pour over the ice cream.

2. Top with the peach lambic, and serve with a long spoon.

> " Beer does not make itself properly by itself. It takes an element of mystery and of things that no one can understand."
> —FRITZ MAYTAG, BREWER

WITTE

Serves 2

We have a pet peeve: There are far too many drinks made with the unfiltered Belgian white ale Hoegaarden that play on the word *ho*. There's the Dirty Ho, which can be a combo of Hoegaarden and raspberry lambic (though variations exist), and the Bloody Ho (Hoegaarden plus tomato juice), and many others with equally dubious nomenclature. We're not going to play that game. No way. Instead, this sweet cocktail made with *witbier* is named for our good pal, the poet Liz Witte, who is all honey . . . and not a ho.

Ice cubes
2 ounces Dumante Verdenoce pistachio liqueur
1½ ounces bourbon
2 ounces honey
12 ounces Hoegaarden *witbier*
2 lemon wedges, for garnish

1. Fill a cocktail shaker halfway full with ice cubes. Add the pistachio liqueur, bourbon, and honey and shake until chilled.

2. Strain into two pilsner glasses and top with the Hoegaarden. Garnish each with a lemon wedge and serve.

ROOT **BEER** FLOAT

Serves 2

We specify vanilla ice cream in this grown-up take on the classic soda-fountain dessert, but we also like using a malt-flavored ice cream that we can get locally. Malt happens to be a key ingredient in beer, so it's a natural combination of flavors. Cassis lambic is flavored with black currants.

4 ounces Root liqueur or root beer schnapps
12 ounces cassis lambic
4 scoops vanilla ice cream

Add half of the liqueur and half of the lambic to each of two chilled parfait glasses. Top each with two scoops of ice cream and serve immediately.

" Fill with mingled cream and amber, I will drain that glass again. Such hilarious visions clamber through the chambers of my brain. Quaintest thoughts—queerest fancies, come to life and fade away. What care I how time advances? I am drinking ale today."
—EDGAR ALLAN POE

THE **RETIREE**
Serves 2

We envision this as a Belgian-influenced Tiki drink. Maybe you can sip these while sitting on your porch in Boca Raton on a balmy afternoon after a round of golf with your pals from the condo association. But you don't have to wait until you're 65 to enjoy one of these—retire early! We make ours with Kasteel Rouge, a high-alcohol Belgian brown ale flavored with sour cherries. It's decadent, but you've worked hard. You deserve it. If you can't find Kasteel Rouge, try using Vichtenaar, Monk's Cafe, or Liefmans Oud Bruin.

Crushed ice
10 ounces Kasteel Rouge
2 ounces white rum
1 ounce vodka
1½ ounces blue curaçao
2 ounces pineapple juice
2 pineapple wedges, for garnish
4 maraschino cherries, for garnish

1. Fill two hurricane glasses with crushed ice, and add half of the beer, rum, vodka, curaçao, and pineapple juice to each glass. Stir gently.

2. Add a cocktail umbrella (the biggest one you can find), a wedge of pineapple on the side of each glass, and a couple of maraschino cherries in the drink for garnish. Drink with a straw.

APPALOOSA

Serves 1

The Appaloosa is a great drink to welcome autumn. You'll want to find a Belgian blond abbey ale, like Affligem or Leffe, the fruity notes of which are accentuated by the apple and ginger flavors. Use real apple cider for this, not apple juice or hard cider.

Ice cubes
1 ounce Snap ginger liqueur
1 ounce Aperol
1½ ounces apple cider
Juice of 1 lemon
4 ounces blond abbey ale
2 ounces seltzer
1 apple wheel, for garnish

1. Fill a cocktail shaker halfway full with ice cubes. Combine the ginger liqueur, Aperol, cider, and lemon juice in the shaker and shake to combine.

2. Strain into a 12-ounce pilsner glass. Top with the ale and seltzer. Cut a notch in the apple wheel, place it on the rim of the glass, and serve.

SING SING SLING

Serves 1

The Sing Sing Sling is adapted from a recipe by our friend Fred Thompson, author of *Bourbon, Hot Chocolate*, and other books about health food.

Ice cubes
2 ounces bourbon
½ ounce vanilla simple syrup (see page 19)
Juice of 1 lime
1 tablespoon blueberry compote or preserves
4 ounces cassis lambic
2 fresh blueberries, for garnish

1. Fill a cocktail shaker halfway full with ice cubes. Add the bourbon, syrup, lime juice, and blueberry preserves, and shake until well chilled.

2. Strain into a flute glass, and top with the cassis lambic. Garnish with a couple of fresh blueberries, and serve.

" No soldier can fight unless he is properly fed on beef and beer." —JOHN CHURCHILL, FIRST DUKE OF MARLBOROUGH

JOE PÊCHE

Serves 1

Is this drink funny to you? Is it here to amuse you? Well . . .
fine, that's what we want, even if our puns don't always get
the positive response we hope for. In any case, don't think
about the name too hard, just make the drink.

Ice cubes
1½ ounces gin
½ ounce brandy
½ ounce peach liqueur
Dash of freshly squeezed lime juice
5 ounces peach lambic

1. Fill a Collins glass halfway full with ice cubes. Pour the gin,
brandy, peach liqueur, and lime juice into the glass.

2. Top with the lambic, stir gently, and serve.

MYRNA **LOY**

Serves 1

Light, crisp, bubbly, and pleasantly sour, *geuze* is a style of Belgian lambic made from a blend of aged and young beers, and further fermented in the bottle. We love it, though the intense sourness is an acquired taste. The stylish mix of sweet and tart flavors in this drink reminds us of wise-cracking Nora Charles, Loy's great character from the Thin Man detective movies.

Ice cubes
1 ounce Belle de Brillet pear liqueur
½ ounce St. Elizabeth Allspice Dram
½ ounce ginger simple syrup (see page 19)
2 ounces hard cider
3 ounces *geuze*

1. Fill a cocktail shaker halfway full with ice cubes. Add the pear liqueur, allspice dram, and ginger simple syrup and shake to combine.

2. Strain the mixture into a flute glass. Top with the cider.

3. Pour the *geuze* into a separate glass and serve on the side, so that the drinker can top the cocktail with the beer just before consuming.

Nora Charles: How many drinks have you had?
Nick Charles: This will make six martinis.
Nora Charles (to the waiter): All right.
Leo, will you bring me five more martinis?
Line them up right here."
—*THE THIN MAN* (1934)

4

Beyond the Shadow
OF A
STOUT

(OR, MADE TO PORTER)

*Kelso Cola • The Backward Crawl • Stout Sangaree •
Marble Sheep • Oatmeal Cookie • Empress's New Clothes •
Grapefruit Moon • Chocolate Truffle • Chic-Choc •
Black & Tan • Nutter Butter Beer*

Way back when I (Howard) was young, a stout set me on the happy path of beer geekdom. The first beer to enthrall me was Mackeson XXX Milk Stout. Creamy, sweet, and nearly opaque black, this beer seemed more like a luxurious dessert than an alcoholic beverage. After years of trying to comprehend my friends' enthusiasm for beer, Mackeson was a revelation.

In this chapter, you'll find cocktails made with the darkest beers: the stouts and porters. These beers tend to have earthy, roasty notes that play well with sweet ingredients like port and rum.

KELSO **COLA**

Serves 1

This one is adapted from the Holland House Bar & Refuge in Nashville and named after the town where Prichard's is distilled. The Holland House makes their own coffee liqueur, which they use for this drink, but owner Terry Raley helpfully suggested using Tia Maria or Rua Vieja Licor de Café when making this at home. For the stout, Hitachino Nest Espresso Stout is ideal; Goose Island Bourbon County Coffee Stout is also stellar. Play around with coffee stouts that you can find locally.

1½ ounces Prichard's Sweet Lucy bourbon liqueur
¾ ounce spiced rum
½ ounce coffee liqueur
1 egg white
Ice cubes
12 ounces espresso stout

1. Combine the bourbon liqueur, rum, coffee liqueur, and egg white in a shaker without ice. Shake vigorously to blend the ingredients and froth the egg white. Fill the shaker halfway with ice cubes, and then shake some more.

2. Add 1 large ice cube to an old-fashioned glass, and strain the mixture into the glass.

3. Top with the stout. Pour the remaining stout into a pint glass and serve on the side.

NOTE • Please be cautious and use common sense when it comes to serving raw eggs to anyone with a compromised immune system.

THE **BACKWARD** CRAWL

Serves 1

The scarlet ibis is the national bird of Trinidad and Tobago. This flip recalls those sunny islands, with its flavors of coconut and rum, with meringue from the egg. Shake this over ice for a long time in order to properly aerate the egg, then enjoy the light, creamy texture you've created.

Ice cubes
1 egg
1½ ounces coconut syrup
1 ounce Scarlet Ibis rum
2½ ounces porter

1. Fill a cocktail shaker halfway full with ice cubes. Add the egg, syrup, and rum and shake vigorously to aerate the egg. Keep shaking.

2. Strain into a coupe glass, top with the porter, and drink while thinking about the beach.

 NOTE • Please be cautious and use common sense when it comes to serving raw eggs to anyone with a compromised immune system.

STOUT SANGAREE

Serves 2

Sangaree is an Old English name for sangria, which traditionally is made with wine. We like the deep roastiness of stout, balanced by a bit of rich ruby port. A dry Irish stout such as Murphy's or Guinness is a good choice.

2 teaspoons simple syrup (see page 19)
12 ounces stout
2 ounces ruby port
Pinch of freshly grated nutmeg
Pinch of ground cinnamon

1. Pour the simple syrup into a chilled beer mug. Slowly add the stout so that a big foamy head forms at the top of the glass.

2. Float the port on top of the foam by carefully pouring it over the back of a spoon. Sprinkle with the nutmeg and cinnamon, and serve immediately.

> Of doctors and medicines we have in plenty more than enough. What you may, for the love of God, send is some large quantity of beer." —DISPATCH FROM THE COLONY OF NEW SOUTH WALES (AUSTRALIA), 1854

MARBLE SHEEP

Serves 2

This grownups-only sundae highlights the chocolate and espresso flavors in one of our favorite American beers, Founders Breakfast Stout. If you can't find Founders near you, try experimenting with any oatmeal stout you can find. The proportions here are intended as estimates to be adjusted according to your tastes. Fox's U-Bet is our top choice for chocolate syrup, but use whichever brand you prefer. Serve your Marble Sheep with two spoons, and keep the bottle of beer handy to refill as needed. The marbled black and white appearance in the parfait glass is quite lovely!

1 pint vanilla ice cream
12 ounces Founders Breakfast Stout or other oatmeal stout
Chocolate syrup (as much as desired!)

Fill a tall parfait glass three-quarters full with the ice cream. Add about 6 ounces of stout. Drizzle with chocolate syrup and serve with a long spoon. I (Howard) like to discreetly take mine into another room and finish it before anyone asks me to share.

OATMEAL COOKIE

Serves 4

Another dessert cocktail made with oatmeal stout, the Oatmeal Cookie gets a spicy edge from Goldschläger, a Swiss cinnamon schnapps that has thin flakes of gold leaf floating in it.

Ice cubes
3 ounces molasses
3 ounces ruby port
1½ ounces Goldschläger
12 ounces oatmeal stout

1. Fill a cocktail shaker halfway full with ice cubes. Add the molasses, port, and Goldschläger. Shake until cold.
2. Strain into four old-fashioned glasses. Top with the oatmeal stout, and serve.

" Fermentation equals civilization."
—JOHN CIARDI

EMPRESS'S **NEW** CLOTHES

Serves 1

Imperial stouts, also called Russian imperial stouts, are known for their high alcohol content and especially full body. Contrary to the style's name, Russian imperial stout originated in England, where it was brewed for export to the court of Catherine the Great. This stately cocktail balances the alcohol bite of the beer with sweet and herbal notes from the spirits.

Ice cubes
1 ounce bourbon
1 ounce Drambuie
½ ounce Grand Marnier
1 ounce freshly squeezed orange juice
2 ounces Russian imperial stout
Dash of orange bitters

1. Fill a cocktail shaker halfway full with ice cubes. Add the bourbon, Drambuie, Grand Marnier, and orange juice, and shake until cold.

2. Strain into an old-fashioned glass. Top with the imperial stout, add a dash of bitters, and serve.

GRAPEFRUIT MOON

Serves 1

Famed drinks writer Paul Clarke came up with this one, and named it after a weepy old Tom Waits tune from the *Closing Time* album. Paul used Samuel Smith's stellar Oatmeal Stout in his creation, which we wholeheartedly endorse. We also endorse the music of Mr. Waits, pretty much all the time.

Ice cubes
1½ ounces bourbon
1½ ounces freshly squeezed grapefruit juice
1 tablespoon simple syrup (page 19) or maple syrup
3 ounces stout

1. Fill a cocktail shaker halfway full with ice cubes. Add the bourbon, juice, and syrup, and shake well.

2. Fill a pilsner glass with crushed ice, and strain the mixture into the glass. Top with the stout, and serve.

> You can't be a real country unless you have a beer and an airline—it helps if you have some kind of a football team, or some nuclear weapons, but at the very least you need a beer." —FRANK ZAPPA

CHOCOLATE **TRUFFLE**

Serves 2

When we say to add the stout slowly here, we mean it. Add it too fast and you'll get way too much of a head. Young's Double Chocolate Stout is a very rich, full-bodied beer, and the classic English chocolate stout.

8 ounces Lindemans Framboise (raspberry lambic)
12 ounces Young's Double Chocolate Stout
4 fresh raspberries

1. Add half of the lambic to each of two goblets, then slowly top with equal portions of the chocolate stout.

2. Garnish each goblet with a couple of fresh raspberries, and serve.

❝ Fermentation may have been a greater discovery than fire." —DAVID RAINS WALLACE

CHIC-CHOC

Serves 2

Few cured meat products ignite people's passion quite the way bacon does. We've seen it incorporated into chocolate bars, peanut brittle, hot sauces, and, yes, even cocktails. The bacon-and-beverage combo isn't as odd as it may sound at first; in the world of dark beers, smoke has been used as a flavoring for centuries. *Rauchbier* (literally "smoked beer") is a German style made by drying the malt over an open flame, imparting it with savory smoky flavoring and a strong aroma reminiscent of bacon. This recipe combines three winning flavors: sweet chocolate, roasted chicory, and salty bacon. It's adapted from a drink served at the Dogfish Head Craft Brewery in Delaware.

1 thick slice bacon
8 ounces semisweet chocolate chips
Ice cubes
1½ ounces chocolate vodka
1½ ounces Root liqueur (or another root beer schnapps)
12 ounces Dogfish Head Chicory Stout

1. Cook the bacon slice until crisp; when cool, cut in half and place on a piece of waxed paper.

2. Melt the chocolate chips in the microwave in 15-second intervals, stirring until they are evenly melted. Drizzle the melted chocolate over the bacon pieces and let set.

3. Fill a cocktail shaker halfway full with ice cubes. Add the vodka and Root, and shake to combine.

4. Strain the mixture into two large cocktail glasses. Top with equal amounts of the stout, and lay one chocolate-covered bacon strip over each glass.

BLACK & TAN

Serves 4

The Black & Tan is probably the best known of all the beer cocktails. Its striking appearance comes from a layering of two beers, which according to British tradition should be Guinness Stout and either Harp Lager or Bass Ale. A good bartender will be skilled at making this drink from draft, but you can also make it at home. You float the stout over the lager by pouring it into the glass slowly, over the back of a spoon. Be sure to use one of the Guinness cans, with the nitrogen capsule inside, rather than a bottle. Your resulting drink will have a dramatic, two-colored presentation.

8 ounces Harp Lager or Bass Ale
8 ounces Guinness Stout

Pour the lager carefully into a pint glass (you don't want to create a head). Slowly and carefully, pour the Guinness over the back of a spoon into the glass, on top of the lager. Serve.

 VARIATIONS • Because it's so simple, the Black & Tan is open to nearly limitless variations. Here are some of our favorites.
• *Black & Blue:* Float Guinness on top of Hoegaarden.
• *Black Bart:* Float Guinness on top of cola.
• *Black Castle:* Float Guinness on top of Newcastle Brown Ale.
• *Blacksmith:* Float Guinness on top of Smithwick's Irish Ale.
• *Black Velvet:* Float Guinness on top of champagne.
• *Lava Lamp:* This is your classic Black & Tan, with a splash of Lindemans Framboise on top.

NUTTER BUTTER BEER

Serves 4

Peanut butter doesn't last long in our house. I (Howard) will consume Reese's Peanut Butter Cups exclusively if Ashley is not around to remind me of the existence of other food groups. My passion for peanut inspired this luxurious dessert drink, which stars Castries Peanut Rum Crème, a brilliant rum-based liqueur from St. Lucia. The velvety texture and thick head of the cream stout make these irresistible.

Ice cubes
4 ounces Castries Peanut Rum Crème
4 ounces vanilla simple syrup (page 19)
12 ounces cream stout

1. Fill a cocktail shaker halfway full with ice cubes. Add the Castries and simple syrup and shake well to combine.
2. Strain equally into four old-fashioned glasses. Top each with equal amounts of the cream stout. Stir gently and enjoy.

5

THE DARK

at the End of the Tunnel

(OR, AMBER WAVES OF GRAIN)

Para Todo Bien • The Bishop's Wife • One Sunset • Cold
Storage • Phil Collins • Sleepy Hollow • The Usurper • Fyodor
• Colonial Flip • Monkey Trick • Over the Cuckoo's Nest •
Old Monk's Belly • Sahtiday

The recipes in this chapter call for all the darker beers that are neither stouts nor porters. The flavor profiles vary widely. Some darker beers have caramel and bready notes, others are bracingly bitter, and still others are spiced or sweet. The color of the beer doesn't tell you much about how these beers will taste. Brown ales tend to be mild, medium-bodied, and malty, though American brewers have produced versions that are a bit stronger and hoppier than their English counterparts. Two classic autumn beers, Oktoberfest and pumpkin ale, are darker beers with spices added. Barleywines are intense and quite strong. We suggest specific beers in many of these recipes, but go ahead and play with what's available near you.

PARA **TODO** BIEN

Serves 2

There's an Oaxacan saying that goes, *"Para todo mal, mezcal, y para todo bien también,"* which means "For everything bad, mezcal, and for everything good too." It's a versatile spirit. This drink matches it up with Mexican dark beer and aromatic cilantro.

8 sprigs fresh cilantro
Ice cubes
2 ounces mezcal
1 ounce freshly squeezed lime juice
¾ ounce simple syrup (page 19)
12 ounces Negra Modelo

1. Muddle 6 of the cilantro sprigs in a mixing glass. Add ice cubes, the mezcal, lime juice, and simple syrup. Shake well.

2. Fill two Collins glasses with ice, and strain the mixture into them. Top each with the beer. Garnish with the remaining cilantro sprigs and serve.

THE **BISHOP'S** WIFE

Serves 1

With its cherry accent, this drink reminds us of Black Forest cake. Doppelbocks are strong, dark, and malty German lagers. They are full-bodied and relatively high in alcohol, and can range in color from dark amber to nearly black.

> 2 tablespoons cherry preserves
> 1½ ounces chilled dark rum
> 4 ounces chilled doppelbock
> 1 lime wedge, for garnish

Muddle the cherries with the rum in an old-fashioned glass. Top with the dopplebock, garnish with the lime wedge, and serve.

" Keep your libraries, your penal institutions, your insane asylums—give me beer. You think man needs rule, he needs beer. The world does not need morals, it needs beer. The souls of men have been fed with indigestibles, but the soul could make use of beer." —HENRY MILLER

ONE **SUNSET**
Serves 1

This one is adapted from a drink served at the now-defunct West Hollywood bar of the same name. It's immensely refreshing, thanks to the fruit and mint that accentuate American amber lagers such as those made by Brooklyn Brewery or Cape Ann Brewing Company (we like their Fisherman's Brew).

7 red grapes
10 fresh mint leaves, plus 1 sprig, for garnish
Ice cubes
2 ounces vodka
¾ ounce Aperol
¾ ounce simple syrup (page 19)
½ ounce freshly squeezed lemon juice
1½ ounces amber lager

1. Muddle 6 of the grapes and the mint leaves in a mixing glass. Fill the glass halfway full with ice cubes, then add the vodka, Aperol, simple syrup, and lemon juice, and stir.

2. Strain into a Collins glass, and top with the amber lager. Garnish with the mint sprig and the remaining red grape, and serve.

COLD STORAGE

Serves 1

The deep maltiness of a doppelbock is given an apricot-tinged spotlight in this cool-weather sipper. We enjoy these in the fall, when a solid drink like this helps take the bite out of the chilly air. Naturally, you can experiment by making these with Oktoberfest beers.

2 ounces dark rum
1 ounce apricot liqueur
1 ounce freshly squeezed lime juice
2 tablespoons light brown sugar
5 ounces dark beer

Add the rum, apricot liqueur, lime juice, and brown sugar to an old-fashioned glass, and stir to dissolve the sugar. Top with the beer and serve.

PHIL **COLLINS**

Serves 1

Barleywine is one of those beer styles that folks either hold in the highest esteem or can't fathom how anyone can finish a glass. We respect that this style of ale takes some getting used to. Barleywines are intensely sweet, quite complex, and often bracingly bitter with a high alcohol content. Many craft breweries produce their versions of barleywine in the autumn. We use this singular brew in a variation on a classic cocktail (Phil is Tom's cousin), tempering the hop bite with gin and lemon.

> Ice cubes
> 1 ounce gin
> 1 ounce freshly squeezed lemon juice
> 1 ounce simple syrup (page 19)
> 3 ounces barleywine
> 1 lemon twist, for garnish

Fill a highball glass with a few ice cubes, and add the gin, lemon juice, and simple syrup. Stir gently. Top with the barleywine, garnish with the lemon twist, and serve.

 All other nations are drinking Ray Charles beer and we are drinking Barry Manilow."
—Dave Barry

SLEEPY **HOLLOW**

Serves 1

We have a Stelzer family tradition: Every year for Halloween, we choose some quiet destination, rent a hotel room, and get the heck out of town. One of our favorite trips took us to Sleepy Hollow, the town in upstate New York where Washington Irving's creepy legend is set. This drink, created in honor of Irving's Headless Horseman, is a flip made with pumpkin beer, which is traditionally produced in the fall. You'll have to shake it for a long time over ice in order to properly aerate the egg and get a nice meringue. But don't lose your head— it just takes some practice.

Crushed ice
1 ounce 100-proof rye whiskey
1 ounce apple brandy
½ ounce maple syrup
1 egg
2 ounces pumpkin ale
Freshly grated nutmeg, for garnish

1. Fill a cocktail shaker three-quarters full with crushed ice. Add the whiskey, brandy, maple syrup, and egg, and shake vigorously. Keep shaking.

2. Pour the ale into a tulip glass and strain the contents of the shaker over it. Stir gently. Garnish with a sprinkling of grated nutmeg and serve.

NOTE • Please be cautious and use common sense when it comes to serving raw eggs to anyone with a compromised immune system.

THE **USURPER**

Serves 2

Scotland is known for many wonderful things, like Sean
Connery, Sir Arthur Conan Doyle, the Edinburgh Fringe
festival, and the Incredible String Band, but whisky is
probably the Scottish product we love best. We honor Scotch
whisky by melding it with rich and malty Scottish ale and
herbal, honey-infused Drambuie liqueur.

Ice cubes
2 ounces Scotch whisky
2 ounces Drambuie
12 ounces Scottish ale
2 tarragon sprigs, for garnish

1. Fill a cocktail shaker halfway full with ice cubes. Add the
Scotch and Drambuie, and shake to combine.
2. Strain the mixture into two old-fashioned glasses and top
with equal amounts of the Scottish ale. Garnish each glass with a
sprig of tarragon and serve.

" There is more to life than beer alone, but
beer makes those other things even better."
—STEPHEN MORRIS, *THE GREAT BEER TREK*

FYODOR

Serves 1

Use a dark lager or a German-style *schwarzbier* for this one. Unlike stouts and porters, dark lagers (like Dixie Blackened Voodoo or Samuel Adams Black Lager) aren't necessarily heavy. The style maintains a roasty, nutty flavor, as you might expect from a darker beer, which is complemented wonderfully by the citrus and herbal notes that come from the Becherovka, a Czech bitters.

Ice cubes
½ ounce Becherovka
½ ounce Grand Marnier
½ ounce star anise–infused simple syrup (page 19)
4 ounces dark lager or *schwarzbier*
1 orange twist, for garnish

1. Fill a cocktail shaker halfway full with ice cubes. Add the Becherovka, Grand Marnier, and simple syrup and shake well.

2. Strain into an old-fashioned glass, then add the beer. Twist the orange twist over the drink to get some of the oil in the glass, then drop the twist into the drink. Serve immediately.

COLONIAL **FLIP**
Serves 2

Not a flip in the sense that we know it today (modern flips contain an egg), this one comes from 1700s New England, where barkeepers would serve warm drinks to folks who came inside seeking shelter from the frigid winters. Back then, the drink would be heated with a poker that had been sitting in a fire. You probably don't have a poker handy, but just warm your drink on a stovetop for a similar effect.

10 ounces barleywine
1 ounce unsulfured molasses
2 tablespoons canned pumpkin puree (not pumpkin pie filling)
2 ounces dark rum
2 cinnamon sticks

1. Add the barleywine, molasses, and pumpkin puree to a small saucepan and heat over low heat until warm.

2. Divide the mixture between two mugs. Top each mug with half of the rum. Garnish each with a cinnamon stick and serve.

Beer is proof that God loves us and wants us to be happy." —BENJAMIN FRANKLIN

MONKEY TRICK

Serves 1

This drink was adapted from a recipe given to us by the composer Jonathan Coleclough, who got together with some friends in Reading, England, to experiment with creating some beer cocktails. Their handwritten notes were a bit hard to read, and became harder as the list (and the evening, we presume) went on, but this drink seemed to be the group's favorite. Banana Bread Beer is brewed by Wells & Young's Brewing Company in Bedford. It's malty and medium-bodied, comparable to Newcastle Brown Ale in body and texture, with an inviting bready aroma and subtle spiciness.

¾ ounce crème de banana
1 ounce blackcurrant syrup
8 ounces Banana Bread Beer, slightly chilled

Add the crème de banana and blackcurrant syrup to a chilled double old-fashioned glass and stir to combine. Top with the beer. Stir gently and serve.

OVER THE CUCKOO'S NEST

Serves 1

Next time your nutty pals are over, serve them a few of these and we promise they'll go crazy for 'em. We like using Newcastle Brown Ale, but other brown ales work just fine. Samuel Smith makes a classic Nut Brown Ale, whose maltiness and roasted notes play well with the walnut liqueur. Brooklyn Brown Ale is another good choice, though it's somewhat heavier than its English counterparts. Look for amaretto syrup at specialty markets; Torani and Monin are widely available brands.

1 ounce Nux Alpina walnut liqueur
1 ounce amaretto syrup
8 ounces brown ale

Add the walnut liqueur and amaretto syrup to a chilled Collins glass, then top with the ale. Stir gently and serve.

" Smithers, this beer isn't working, I don't feel any younger or funkier." —Mr. Burns, *The Simpsons*

OLD **MONK'S** BELLY

Serves 2

Even though it has the distinction of being one of the first commercial soft drinks ever produced in America, Moxie's intensely herbal flavor (from gentian root) is quite unlike the sweeter soft drinks that came after it. Imagine a cola flavored with tree bark and thyme, and you're getting close. We love the stuff and raise our glasses in its honor with this cocktail. The pleasing bitterness of Moxie brings out the dark beer's roasty notes and the rum's vanilla undertones. Try making this with New Belgium 1554 or Great Divide Dunkel Weiss.

3 ounces Old Monk rum
6 ounces Moxie
6 ounces dark ale

Pour half of the rum into each of two old-fashioned glasses. Divide the Moxie equally between the glasses. Top each glass equally with the beer. Stir gently and serve immediately.

" In heaven there is no beer. That's why we drink ours here." —FRANKIE YANKOVIC, AMERICA'S POLKA KING

SAHTIDAY

Serves 4

Though new to most American drinkers, sahti is actually one of the oldest styles of beer still being made. The unhopped, unfiltered ale hails from Finland, where it is traditionally flavored with juniper. Modern drinkers may be surprised by its banana notes, which come from strains of wild yeast. The Sahtiday highlights the fruitiness of sahti for a tropical refresher that's perfect for any day of the week. If you can't track down a Finnish sahti, some of the more adventurous American craft breweries are making their own domestic versions, notably Dogfish Head, New Belgium, and Goose Island.

One 8-ounce can pineapple chunks with juice
4 ounces 99 Bananas schnapps
12 ounces chilled sahti

1. Muddle the pineapple chunks with their juice in a cocktail shaker. Add the banana schnapps and stir to blend.

2. Pour into four old-fashioned glasses and top each with equal amounts of the sahti. Serve immediately.

MEASUREMENT EQUIVALENTS

Please note that all conversions are approximate.

LIQUID CONVERSIONS

U.S.	Imperial	Metric
1 tsp.		5 ml
1 tbs.	½ fl oz.	15 ml
2 tbs.	1 fl oz.	30 ml
3 tbs.	1½ fl oz.	45 ml
¼ cup	2 fl oz.	60 ml
⅓ cup	2½ fl oz.	75 ml
⅓ cup + 1 tbs.	3 fl oz.	90 ml
⅓ cup + 2 tbs.	3½ fl oz.	100 ml
½ cup	4 fl oz.	120 ml
⅔ cup	5 fl oz.	150 ml
¾ cup	6 fl oz.	180 ml
¾ cup + 2 tbs.	7 fl oz.	200 ml
1 cup	8 fl oz.	240 ml
1 cup + 2 tbs.	9 fl oz.	275 ml
1¼ cups	10 fl oz.	300 ml
1⅓ cups	11 fl oz.	325 ml
1½ cups	12 fl oz.	350 ml
1⅔ cups	13 fl oz.	375 ml
1¾ cups	14 fl oz.	400 ml
1¾ cups + 2 tbs.	15 fl oz.	450 ml
2 cups (1 pint)	16 fl oz.	475 ml
2½ cups	20 fl oz.	600 ml
3 cups.	24 fl oz.	720 ml
4 cups (1 quart)	32 fl oz.	945 ml
		(1,000 ml is 1 liter)

INDEX

ABOUT **THE** AUTHORS

HOWARD and ASHLEY STELZER are beer enthusiasts and writers. They created the blog ShadowofaStout.com, where one can find all sorts of information about beer and beer cocktails. The Stelzers shared pints of Harpoon IPA on their first date and served Lindemans lambic at their wedding, and they have been learning about, enjoying, and writing about beer ever since. Ashley is a graduate of Le Cordon Bleu and works now as a lifestyle, event, and food photographer and stylist. Howard, a former book publicist, is now a teacher. They live in Cambridge, Massachusetts.